Right Here on This Spot

Sharon Hart Addy

Illustrated by John Clapp

Houghton Mifflin Company
Boston 1999

The text of this book is set in 16-point Adobe Garamond.
The illustrations are watercolor and pencil.

Library of Congress Cataloging-in-Publication Data

Addy, Sharon.
Right here on this spot / by Sharon Hart Addy ; illustrated by John Clapp.
p. cm.
Summary: While digging a ditch in his cabbage field, Grandpa uncovers various items that provide clues to
what has happened in that area of Wisconsin from the time of the Ice Age to the twentieth century.
ISBN 0-395-73091-0
[1. Wisconsin — Antiquities — Fiction. 2. Archaeology — Fiction.] I. Clapp, John, ill. II. Title.
PZ7.A257Ri   1999
[E] — dc20   96-15382 CIP AC

TWP 10 9 8 7 6 5 4 3 2 1
Printed in Singapore

For my parents, Earl and Gerty Hart, who taught me to wonder,
"What happened right here on this spot?"
—S. H. A.

For Mom and Dad
—J. C.

Right here on this spot,
where Grandpa drives a tractor
in his cabbage field,
Indians in ancient times
lit a campfire
on a glacial beach.

They ate mastodon,
chipped stones into tools,
then moved on,
leaving charred wood,
animal bones, and broken stones.

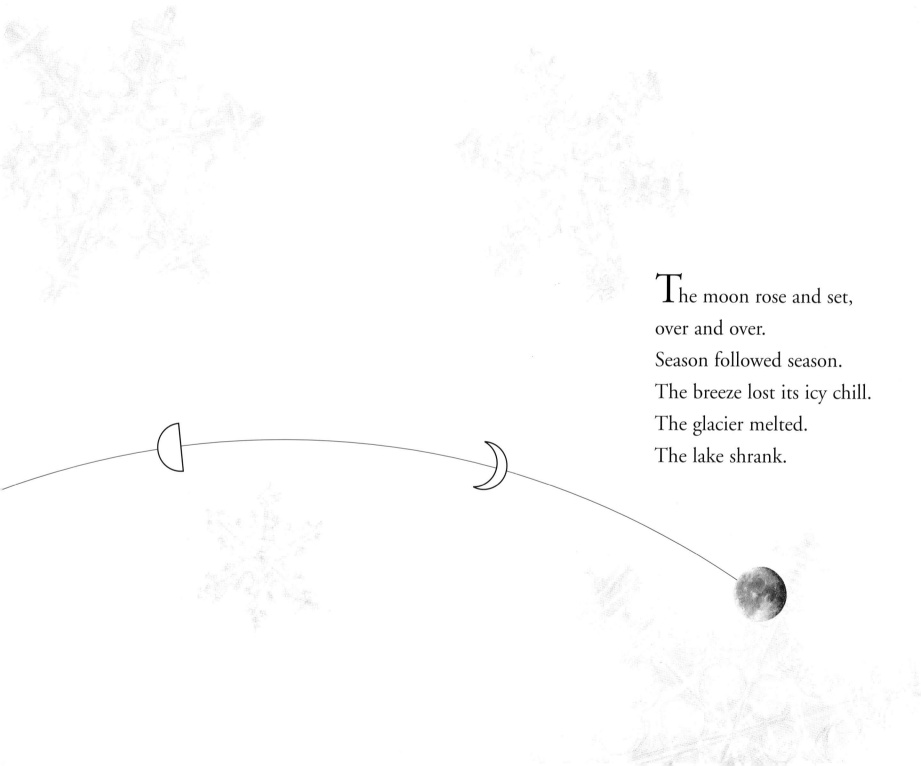

The moon rose and set,
over and over.
Season followed season.
The breeze lost its icy chill.
The glacier melted.
The lake shrank.

The sandy beach remained.
Dusty winds blew over it.
Heavy rains washed it with mud.
Grasses grew.

Trees took root
and rose above the grass.
The trees became a forest.
New animals
called the forest home:
deer, foxes, raccoons,
skunks, squirrels.

New Indians came hunting:
Illinois Indians from the south,
Potawatomi from the north.
Their lost arrowheads
sank into the ground.

Over and over,

fall became winter,

spring became summer,

and fall returned again.

Settlers came.
They cut trees to build a cabin,
pulled stumps to make a field,
and tilled the field
with an ox-drawn plow.

A soldier dressed in blue
lost a button
as he walked the field
before going off to war.
The sun rose and set,
over and over.
Seasons changed.

The cabin became a house.
Barns and fences
spread along the growing fields.
Cows, pigs, and chickens
mooed, grunted, and cackled.

The ancient Indian campfire,
the arrowheads,
and the button
rested in the ground—
a hidden history—

while on the surface,
families worked the fields,
plowing, planting, harvesting.
Farmers left the farm
to their children.
The children grew old
and left it to their children.

Grandpa was digging a ditch
when he found the button.
He took it to Grandma.
She'd never seen the likes of it.

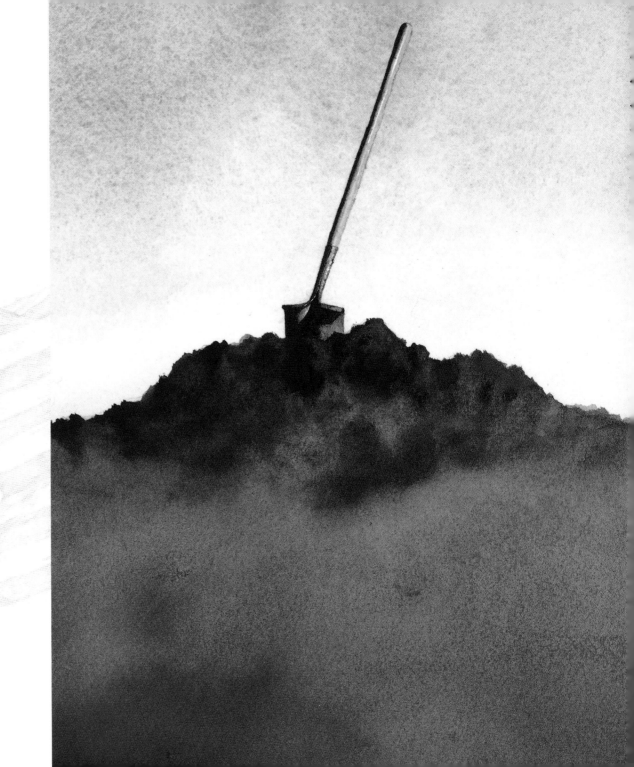

She put it on the windowsill
to show her friend
who sells antiques.
"It's old," Grandma's friend said.
"Civil War."

Arrowheads appeared next,
then sand and a bone—
a bone buried deeper
than a dog would dig,
a bone too big
to be from a deer.

Grandma told her friend,
who called an archaeologist.
He dug very carefully
and studied what he found.

So now we know about
the Civil War soldier
who lost a button,
the Illinois and Potawatomi
who hunted deer,
and the ancient Indians
who warmed themselves
at a campfire—

right here on this spot,
where Grandpa drives a tractor
in his cabbage field.

Historical Note

Paleo-Indians, the ancient Indians of this story, lived during the Ice Age, 13,500 to 9,500 years ago. Their camps have been found along rivers and lakes, places where animals came for water. Paleo-Indian hunters traveled in bands, following herds of mastodon, woolly mammoth, and other large animals. They hunted with spears; the tips were chipped from fine-grained stone. They found the stone along streambeds. If there was none to be found, they traveled great distances or traded with other bands to get it.

As the glaciers of the Ice Age melted, the world of the Paleo-Indians changed. In the area near the southwestern tip of Lake Michigan, where this story is set, the lake shrank, leaving behind old beaches and creating a series of new ones. As the changes took place the Indians adapted, and the woods and hills became home to their descendants.

Hundreds and hundreds of years later, trappers and frontiersmen came to Wisconsin. By the late 1830s, warfare and treaties secured the land along the southwestern shore of Lake Michigan for homesteaders. The homesteads grew to become the acres of farmland we see today spreading out from houses and barns.